This book is dedicated  to Catherine,

the girl who wanted to "love

Blue-Grey Eyes

I searched for answers

In blue-grey eyes.

I scanned the molten reflections

And beguiling shadows,

Chasing the moonbeams in your eyes

To find the starlight

In your soul.

I have kissed your lips,

Gazed into your eyes,

And been lost

Ten thousand times.

Your face

Haunted my dreams

Through the mists of time.

Fate cheated us

Of the lifetime of loving

Which was rightfully ours.

Things the reader should know.

The Norman Conquest took place in 1066 when William the Conqueror defeated the Saxon King Harold at the battle of Hastings.

The French Normans took control of all England and William the Conqueror gave land to all those knights and members of his family who had helped him.

The Crusades were holy wars between the Christians and Muslims. They fought over the control of the Holy Land known today as Israel. In particular the cities of Jerusalem and Bethlehem were important for Christians to visit on a pilgrimage.

Richard I called the Lionheart or Coeur de Leon in French, became King of England in 1192 when his father Henry II died. Richard was called the Lionheart because of his bravery in battle.

Saracen was a name used to describe Muslims' from Syria.

Biddulph and Knypersley are places to the north of Stoke on Trent in Staffordshire.

There is some truth about the Dark Men of Biddulph but no one can prove where they came from. Some say that they are descended from Gypsies. But the myth about Saracen ancestors has persisted.

Alured or Alfred Fitz Ormius was a real person who was Lord of the Manor of Knypersley.

Hakim is a fictional character but it is a matter of some conjecture that a Saracen did indeed return from the Crusades to Biddulph Moor.

The Cloud lies to the north of Biddulph Moor. From the top on a clear day, you can see: - To the north Macclesfield and Alderley Edge. To the north east and east is the Peak District National Park. To the south east lie Rudyard Lake and the Roaches. To the west are the Peckforton Hills and beyond them, Snowdon, the highest Mountain in Wales. To the south west is Briedon Hill in Shropshire. All of the Cheshire plain lies at your feet. It is a short sharp climb to the summit of The Cloud, but well worth the effort for the magnificent view.

Alderley Edge is a place in Cheshire to the north of Biddulph, the land is owned by the National Trust and can be visited free of charge.

Nowadays, rich footballers from Manchester live in large houses, close to Alderley Edge.

The legend of Alderley Edge and the sleeping knights is a well known local story.

The Knights Templar was a society of Knights formed in Jerusalem around 1118. They were persecuted and ceased to exist in 1312, although rumoured to continue to exist as a secret organisation.

Richard De Hastings, was a Master of the Knights Templar.

The Holy Grail is reputed to be either, the vessel which Jesus Christ drank from at the Last Supper or the vessel which Mary Magdalene used to catch Christ's blood when he was crucified. There is no proof it ever existed.

There is no evidence at all that the Teutonic Knights have any kind of secret Chapter which seeks the Holy Grail. They are a Catholic religious order which was founded in 1190 and exists to this day.

Albert de Louvain was indeed a real character from around the time the story is set and is believed to have been killed by three Germanic knights in November 1192 in the woods outside Reims. He did attend the third Crusade but the rest is pure fiction.

The Dark Men of Biddulph Moor

There is a place in Staffordshire,
Just to the north of Stoke,
Where, the local inhabitants
Don't resemble other folk.
There exists a bloodline
For many generations pure,
I refer of course,
To The Men O'Biddle Muir.
'Tis a whispered legend,
They came from far off lands,
A land of burning sun
And shifting desert sands.
No one knows the truth,
The hidden facts elusive.
Scientific tests
Have been, inconclusive.
But there is no doubting,
The evidence is stark,
It cannot be denied,
Those Biddulph men are dark.

HWE Siviter Jan 2010

The news of the Lionheart's crusade to free the Holy Land came late to the Staffordshire wastelands. It wasn't until Alured's eldest brother Robert returned from paying his annual homage to his master at Stafford castle that Alured heard of the great adventure.

Robert de Stafford had left a month since with an entourage of knights, men at arms, his squire and servants to join King Richard at Folkestone. Stafford Castle had been left in the safe keeping of Robert de Stafford's wife Basilla.

Sir Robert de Stafford was an elderly knight three score years or more old and the journey was not an easy undertaking for a man of much younger years but he saw it as his duty to free Jerusalem from the clutches of the Infidel Saladin.

Alured was well aware that as the youngest of four brothers even though his father had been a well respected knight, and that his Grandfather Richard the Forrester had served The Conqueror as standard bearer at Hastings, he himself would have to find his own way in the world and could not rely on much of an inheritance. The Darlestone estates were rich but not rich enough to support four sons and if he remained under his brother's protection on the family estates he would never be a knight and never have a title. Alured's eldest brother had inherited the title Fitz Ormius de Darlestone on the death of their father some two years earlier.

What options were open to him, a young man of stout heart who yearned for adventure? Surely this was the opportunity he had been waiting for. If he could go to the Holy Land on this Crusade, through brave deeds he could carve a name and a place for himself in the world. The only other option open to him was to take Holy Orders

He had developed a strong arm by working hard on his father's estates and as the youngest of four brothers had learned early on how to look after himself. He was proficient both with the long bow and the stave and had mastered the rudiments of swordsmanship in long hours of practice with his brothers. He had grown from boyhood into a man strong in arm and of good health due to the hard work and fresh air he got whilst doing more than his share on the land.
His horsemanship was developed from hunting boar in the woods and wolves which always threatened the livestock on the Estate. He practised regularly with the longbow and was tutored by an old Welshman who had lived on the estate for many years.

Alured decided that he would seek his brothers blessing and set forth on this great adventure as soon as possible. He hoped that his eldest brother Robert would allow him to go.

That evening Alured seized his chance. "Robert I seek your permission to accompany King Richard on the Crusade to free the Holy Land."
"Brother that would be folly, much danger lies in that plan and many, better equipped than you for the hardships, will never survive to see England again. Besides I need you here to help me run the estates"

"But Robert it will not be for long surely, the power and courage of the King will soon overcome all opposition and we will return to this land with great fortunes and reputation. It is after all a Holy quest. Brother I beg you to spare me from my duties here. You have Edward and Thomas to assist you. The harvest is gathered in and it has been a plentiful year and soon when you kill and salt the beasts and the swine there will be little for me to do here other than to hunt boar and deer."

"Very well Alured if you must persist with this folly I cannot deny you. It is my duty as your elder brother and as one who loves you, to equip you the best way I can, to face the perils you will undoubtedly meet. I will give you a riding horse and a pack horse. I will provide you with a coat of mail and enough money to pay for your food and passage across the sea to France and beyond to the Holy Land. I can do no more than this other than to give you a recommendation to our Liege Lord Robert de Stafford in the hope that he will take you under his patronage when you reach the Holy Land. May you bring honour to our family name. I'm certain that you are made of the right stuff and will not let us down. Now brothers all, let us drink a toast to the success of this Crusade and pray for the safe return of our youngest brother"

Thus it was that Alured set forth the very next morning on his great adventure to the Holy Land to fight for King Richard the Lionheart. He was full of expectation and very keen to prove himself worthy of the faith his brothers had shown in him.

STAFFORD CASTLE

2nd Chapter
The Journey from Darlestone to Calais

Alured rose before first light and set off before dawn the next morning with the best wishes of his three brothers ringing in his ears. He had chosen his favourite hunting horse a brave and fiery stallion and a steady mare for his pack animal. He was armed with a coat of mail which had belonged to his late father and his brother also gave him his late father's sword. He had a good yew bow and a quiver full of arrows with heads designed for hunting both beast and man. A scroll of recommendation hastily drawn up the night before by the local priest and signed with his mark from his illiterate brother Robert. Most importantly his brother also gave him a purse containing enough money, if he was frugal, to keep body and soul together until he reached the Holy Land. He headed first to Stafford Castle to gain news of where and how he could follow Robert de Stafford's footsteps and join King Richard's army.

On arrival at Stafford Castle the news was not encouraging. It seemed that Robert de Stafford had departed not a month ago but some three months since in the month of July and was by now across France and more likely than not already in the Holy Land or at least Messina in Sicily where many Crusader ships stopped over.

So it was with the optimism of youth that Alured left Stafford behind and struck east towards where the great stone castle at Tameworth was being built by Robert Marmion, surely he would gain some useful intelligence there.

First Alured had to pass through Lichfield and he was amazed at the size and magnificence of the Norman Cathedral which he found being built in the centre of the busy town. He purchased some bread and cheese from the market place and a jug of ale to wash it down. He did not tarry long as he wanted to make Tameworth before nightfall and still had some hard miles through the forest to travel. However he did find time to go down on his knees in front of the unfinished Cathedral to ask God for success in his quest.

At last after a long, hard day in the saddle Alured arrived at the huge stonework's of Tameworth Castle being thrown up in a bend of the river. Already the great keep was taking shape and stonemasons were at work on the foundations of a gate house. Meanwhile gangs of labourers worked on the mighty earthworks which marked the beginnings of the curtain walls. It was impressive indeed to one such as Alured who had never ventured further than the wooden motte and bailey constructed at Stafford. As he approached along the river bank he wondered how long the castle would take to finish. He also marvelled at the wealth it must take to employ so many artisans and workmen for so many years. Alured had thought that the Norman Cathedral at Lichfield was impressive but that was being built to worship God, this castle had a very different purpose.

He now looked for lodgings but as the small town was full to bursting with workers and their families and being unable to find anywhere to sleep decided to sleep in the shelter of the footings of the gate house. Hobbling his horses so that they would be able to graze but not stray far he then wrapped himself in his thick woollen cloak and settled down for the night.

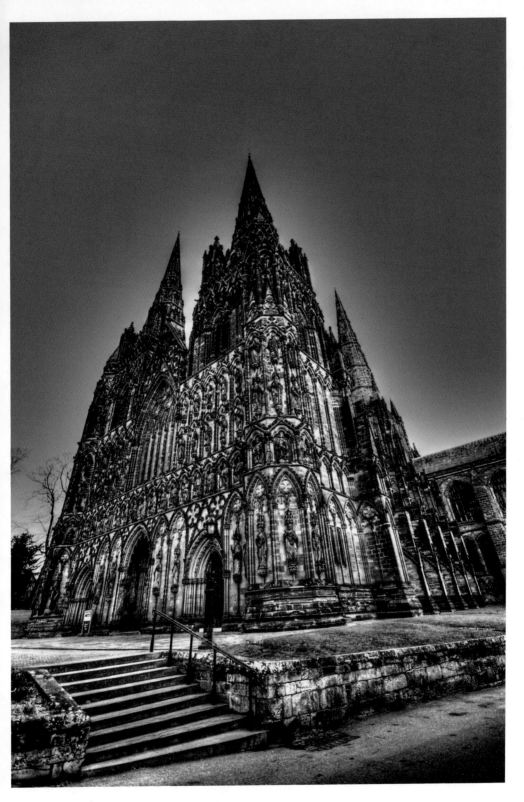

LICHFIELD CATHEDRAL

He awoke next morning before dawn, cold and stiff and decided after a meagre breakfast of left over bread and cheese, to press on from Tameworth with all haste towards the port of Dover.

TAMWORTH CASTLE

Alured headed south towards the town of Warwick on the banks of the river Avon where the Conqueror had built one of the earliest castles to be constructed in England and stronghold of the powerful Beaumont family. The new stone built shell keep replacing the old wooden motte and bailey had only been completed a few years before and was an impressive symbol of Norman Angevin power. Alured hoped he would glean some useful information at the castle if he could gain an audience with the Duke.

For two nights Alured rode hard and camped in the woods at night.
As he approached Warwick along the banks of the Avon he realised that Stafford and Tameworth castles were small by comparison and that this castle commanded views of the countryside for miles around and the defensive position chosen on a sandstone bluff in a bend of the river Avon made this an impressive stronghold which would be easily defended. In short it was an excellent seat of power for a very eminent Norman Duke.
Unfortunately when Alured arrived at the castle the gates had been shut for the night and would not be opened until the following morning. So once again Alured slept another night in the open. The following morning he presented himself at the castle and waited in line for an audience with the Reeve. It soon came to his attention that the Duke of Warwick had also headed with a strong force of men at arms and foot soldiers for the Crusade. It was pointless hanging around waiting for more old news so feeling somewhat stupid for wasting so much valuable time Alured resolved that he would ride immediately for the Channel ports and not waste further time on fruitless enquiries.

Eventually reaching Dover some days later Alured managed to secure passage on a ship for himself and his horses to the port of Calais.

WARWICK CASTLE

3rd Chapter
Alured's Adventures in France

I met a Lady in the meads
Full beautiful, a faery's child,
Her hair was long, her foot was light,
And her eyes were wild.

The crossing to France was a rough one and Alured not having been further than a few miles from his North Staffordshire home before, experienced his first ever bout of sea sickness. The rough sailors laughed and patted him on the back as he hung over the side of the vessel with a face as green as the sea itself. Luckily his horses were better sailors and seemed none the worse for their time at sea.

At last the ship reached Calais and Alured was very relieved to set foot on dry land again. Saddling up his horse and loading the pack horse he was soon on his way through the town of Calais and on southwards.

This northern part of France was very much like England heavily wooded with occasional small villages and strips of open fields where the peasants toiled for their Lord. There were swineherds with pigs in the forest making the most of the autumn bounty of acorns which the pigs gobbled up greedily. Alured knew that it wouldn't be long before the unfortunate creatures were turned into meat and salted in barrels for the long winter to come.

The thought of a long winter hastened Alured as he was determined to reach the Mediterranean Sea before the winter gales set in. One bout of seasickness was quite enough and Alured dreaded setting foot on board a ship again.

Occasionally Alured came upon a small town and managed to buy bread and a little goat's cheese to supplement his meagre rations. It was in one of these towns Dreux, that he was approached by a young woman of around his own age. She was slender and pale faced with flowing chestnut coloured hair and huge blue/grey eyes which examined his face closely before she spoke.

"Excuse me sire I know you are a stranger to these parts, may I ask you from whence you came?" Alured was taken aback as he did not expect to be addressed in perfect English by this girl.
"I am from England, from Staffordshire; can I be of some service to you?"
"My brother has gone to the Crusade and I am following to try and find him. If as I think, you too are headed towards the Holy Land, I wonder if I may travel with you? My horse and money were stolen by ruffians in the forest a few miles from here and I have lived for weeks on the charity of the Church and what scraps I can beg from the townspeople."

"Madam as much as it grieves me my answer must be no. I am in a hurry to make the port of Marseilles before the winter storms prevent sailing."

"But sire I would not slow you down and besides I can make myself useful, I can make a fire and cook and have other skills besides."

"What other skills do you speak of?"

"Lend me your bow sire and I will demonstrate."

Alured was fascinated that this slender girl thought that she could use his bow. It was not a weapon that a woman would ever have the strength to use let alone this wisp of a girl. It was a sturdy length of yew and took a powerfully built man to draw it with any effect.

He nodded his assent and she took the bow from his pack horse and within seconds had bent the yew and strung the bow. Then selecting a broad bladed hunting arrow from Alured's quiver she searched for a target. Selecting a birch sapling not two spans wide, some 60 yards away she took up a practiced sideways stance and fitting the notch of the arrow into the nock. To Alured's astonishment she drew the bow and released the arrow with hardly a second to take aim. Amazingly the arrow buried itself into the middle of the trunk of the birch tree with a satisfying 'thwack' and the girl turned to smile at Alured before strolling over to recover the arrow. When she retrieved the arrow she returned to Alured.

The surprise on his face was obvious and she waited for his verdict on her skills.

"I didn't think you would even manage to draw the bow let alone hit your target," he admitted graciously. "Where does a young maiden such as you learn a skill like that?"

"My mother died bearing me, so from a young age I ran wild in the woods with my father and brother learning to hunt and live off the land. Our family had been dispossessed of our lands by the Norman overlord Humphrey de Highclere and my father declared an outlaw. So we had to live off our wits in the forest until we were restored to our rightful heritage by King Henry. It was that which made my brother decide to join the Crusade but shortly after he left my father died and the Lord demanded that I marry his youngest son to remain under his protection. So I followed my brother's footsteps as I had no wish to marry."

"What do they call you?"

"My name is Catherine. Catherine de Riche, from Hampshire."

"Well fair Catherine I am Alured and I would be pleased to travel with you as a companion and offer you my protection on our way to the Holy Land. Perhaps we should find a bowyer in this town and get you a bow and some arrows of your own?"

"Sire I would be forever in your debt."

So it was that Alured gained a travelling companion for his journey to the Holy Land. He found a bowyer in the town and besides buying a bow and some arrows from a fletcher, he also purchased a thick cloak for the girl to protect her from the chilly approach of winter. She rode astride his pack horse like a man and proved herself to be a more than capable horsewoman.

At night when they stopped to eat and rest she gathered firewood and proved that she could hunt and forage for food. They talked of many things and Alured had never met anyone like her before and started to grow fond of her and value her companionship.

Then one frosty morning as they made their way towards Rocamadour in the limestone gorges full of oak below the monastery; they were set upon by a band of French cutthroats. Catherine was knocked from her horse and stunned. Alured charged his horse towards her assailants and drawing his sword took off the raised arm of one as his horse trampled another under foot. The third grabbed Alured's reins and swiftly drew the horse to the ground trapping Alured's leg beneath the fallen animal. Now the cutthroat raised his cudgel and began to beat the trapped Alured aiming vicious blows at his head. Suddenly the man staggered and dropped his weapon. A strange gurgling noise escaped from his throat. As the man fell to the ground clutching his throat, Alured could see Catherine with her bow in hand not ten yards away and it was then that he realised that the thief had an arrow straight through his neck. Alured freed himself from under his steed and looked around for the other two. The one with no hand and forearm was scurrying away into the woods clutching his stump desperately trying to staunch the flow of blood. The other who had been trampled by Alured's horse was still unconscious.

Alured then noticed that Catherine had a nasty gash on the side of her head and she was looking distinctly shaky on her feet. Rushing to her side Alured picked her up and put her down with her back resting against a huge oak. Taking water from his hog skin he bathed the wound on Catherine's head and examining it carefully he decided that it was just a cut nothing more sinister and would not appear as a scar as it was well above her hairline and would be hidden by her thick lustrous chestnut hair.
"Thank you for rescuing me Catherine I think I was about to get my head mashed and if it wasn't for your skill with the bow I don't like to think of what might have happened."
"Think nothing of it, if it wasn't for you Alured I would still be begging for food back in Dreux. I am glad that I have started to repay your kindness to me."
"No payment is necessary; you have been a much valued travelling companion Catherine. If it wasn't for your skills in finding food I would probably have had many miserable hungry nights with nothing in my belly. Besides I have enjoyed your company."
Alured lifted Catherine onto his horse and mounted behind her putting his arms around her to support her. He secretly enjoyed her close proximity and she did too. It felt good to have his strong arms around her.

ROCAMADOUR

They travelled in this way for two more days and in that time they became even closer sharing more than just the warmth of the campfire and both of them experiencing love for the first time.

They made their way through Cahors with its Pont de Valentre spanning the river Lot and then to Toulouse. From there they rode to Narbonne and east along the coast until they reached Marseilles.

PONT VALENTRE CAHORS

On reaching Marseilles they found the town bustling and full of Crusaders from many Christian lands. Alured made enquiries at many places in the town seeking news of Catherine's brother all to no avail, until one afternoon when entering the harbour area to make further enquiries Catherine spotted a familiar figure arguing with a crusty old sea captain on the harbour wall.

"It's Richard my brother, Richard! Richard! It's me Catherine."

Turning to face her Richard could hardly believe his eyes, seeing his sister here in Marseille was the last thing he expected.

"Catherine dear sister what on earth are you doing here, and who is this stranger with you?" Richard eyed Alured suspiciously.

"Richard this is my friend Alured he has gallantly escorted me across France to find you."

"But what of father Catherine, does he know you are here?"

"I'm sorry Richard but our Father died of the ague shortly after you left. Then that nasty Humphrey de Highclere tried to make me marry his youngest son Ichabod so I ran away to try and find you."

"Well you are here now Catherine and I shall take you to the Holy Land with me and find you the protection of a noble lady when we get there. Now I believe I owe this man a debt which will be difficult to repay. You sire have delivered safely to me, that which I hold dearer than life itself and I shall never forget your service."

"Think nothing of it sir for if it had not been for your sister's skill with a bow and her expert foraging for sustenance I doubt I would be here now."

"Come Catherine and you too sir I will take you to my lodging. You look as if a good meal would do you no harm."

So Alured accompanied Richard and Catherine to an inn where they were fed better than they had been for weeks on a delicious fish stew the likes of which Alured had never tasted before.
Over the next few days Catherine and Alured grew more distant and try as he might Alured could not recapture the closeness they had in the forest. Catherine was after all a lady of good breeding and was bound by strict rules of propriety. Her brother would never understand how close she and Alured had become in the forest and she had no wish to harm the relationship she had with her brother nor endanger the respect he had for Alured. She secretly hoped that Alured would know that she was desperately in love with him and that he would seek her out on his return from Jerusalem

With a heavy heart Alured was under the misimpression that Catherine did not have strong feelings for him and so he decided to bid her and her brother farewell and take a ship immediately for Cyprus. He hoped the heat of battle would help him to forget the idyllic nights they had shared in the forest.

He found a ship bound for Messina and after saying his farewells to Catherine and Richard he embarked on the next part of his journey, hoping beyond hope that this voyage across the Mediterranean would prove smoother and less challenging to the strength of his stomach.
On arrival in Sicily Alured was amazed to discover that he had caught up with the army of the Lionheart and sought to make himself known to Robert de Stafford. On presenting his credentials to his Lord Alured found that Robert was prepared to allow him to fight as a man at arms and was prepared to offer him patronage in memory of his friendship with Alured's father.
Alured soon learned that plans were being laid for the Lionheart's army to sail to Acre as the next leg of the Crusade.

Unfortunately the fleet was dispersed by storms and some of the ships had been wrecked and others sought refuge off the coast of Cyprus. Survivors including Richard I sister had been taken prisoner by a despot called Issac Komnenos.

On the 1st of May Richard arrived at Limassol and demanded that the prisoners be released. Komnenos refused so Richard disembarked his army and decided to take Limassol.

This was Alured's first taste of battle and although the defending army offered little resistance he acquitted himself bravely in combat and Robert de Stafford had cause to take notice of his bravery. Robert had become isolated in the heat of a mêlée and Alured had ridden to his rescue and had beaten off several attackers when it looked as if the elderly knight would be overwhelmed. However Robert's gratitude did not extend to a knighthood for his protector.
Richard Coeur de Leon then found it necessary to take the whole of the island of Cyprus into his control. During a swift campaign Alured saw more skirmishes and always his bravery and skill in battle were apparent.
Then when the island was finally conquered Richard and his army sailed for Acre on June 5th.
Fortunately for the sake of Alured's 'mal de mer' the short crossing was in a smooth sea and he arrived in Acre feeling none the worse for the experience.

Disembarking from the ship Alured was intrigued by the strange vibrant sights and smells of this foreign port. Arabian merchants entered the city to trade not only frankincense and myrrh but also spices, gold, ivory, pearls, precious stones, and textiles—all of which arrived at the port from Africa, India, and the Far East. This trade had been continuous since Roman occupation of the Holy land. Alured wandered along the harbour where strange craft of all kinds from many different lands were waiting to transport cargo all over the Mediterranean.

It was here that Alured had his first unhappy meeting with a grumpy dromedary from an Arab caravan. Not many people are aware of how exactly a camel can spit. Most imagine that a camel spits in the same way that a human spits saliva. Alured found out to his cost that unlike a human, camels actually regurgitate partially digested food from their stomach and fling it from their mouth with a flick of their neck. In this way Alured found himself covered from head to waist with the watery green residue of alfalfa it had been digesting. This was a source of some amusement to onlookers and Alured never did trust camels from that day on.

4th Chapter
1191 The Holy Land near Acre

Look in upon the battle; and in the mist
Was many a noble deed, many a base,
And chance and craft and strength in single fights,
And ever and anon with host to host
Shocks, and the splintering spear, the hard mail hewn,
Shield-breakings, and the clash of brands, the crash
Of battleaxes on shatter'd helms, and shrieks
After the Christ, of those who falling down
Look'd up for heaven, and only saw the mist;
And shouts of heathen and the traitor knights,
Oaths, insult, filth, and monstrous blasphemies,
Sweat, writhings, anguish, labouring of the lungs
In that close mist, and cryings for the light,
Moans of the dying, and voices of the dead.

Alfred, Lord Tennyson from "The Passing of Arthur"

In the heat of the fighting Alured saw the knight attacked and unhorsed by three Saracens. The knight raised himself to one knee and parried the first blow from a Saracen scimitar with his raised shield, but it looked as if the second and third assailants now had an opening to skewer the Crusader with their spears under the raised shield.

With a piercing cry Alured charged at the infidels and diverted them from their intended slaughter. They hesitated and turned to face Alured and that hesitation proved to be their fatal mistake.

The knight recovered his wits and the split second that Alured's advance provided, enabled him to deal a mortal blow to one of the Saracens. The bullocking charge of Alured and the point of his halberd took care of the second Saracen and the third lost heart and fled.

This was a minor skirmish, a prelude to the siege of Acre, but however insignificant in the great scheme of things, it would have certainly cost the Crusader his life, had it not been for Alured's timely assault.

"Sir, I thank you for your aid in my defence. Had it not been for your assistance I doubt that I would have survived," declared the Knight.
"Sire it was nothing and I'm certain that if the roles had been reversed you would have done the same," replied Alured.
"Whom do I have the honour of addressing?" enquired the Knight.
"Sire, I am Alured Fitz Ormius from the wastelands of North Staffordshire."
"Well Alured it is a happy day that we met, and you have rendered me a service that I will ensure will be well rewarded."
"Sire I thought not of reward."

The knight took off his helmet and Alured could see from the noble face that this was no ordinary knight. This was obviously a man of great importance.

"Allow me to introduce myself Alured Fitz Ormius, I am a descendant of the Conqueror and as such directly related to The Lionheart your sovereign King. My name is Roger De Montgomery."

Alured immediately knelt before the knight.
"Forgive me Sire for not showing you the proper deference," pleaded Alured.
"Rise up, it is I who should kneel before you Alured, I owe you my undying gratitude. Tonight you shall dine and rest under my banner in the camp at Acre," promised the Knight. "Come we shall ride together and you shall tell me more of your family. I am sure I once met your father when I was visiting my kinsman Robert, at Stafford Castle."
"Indeed Sire, that is possible as my father is a sokeman of Robert De Stafford."
"Your father is a knight if I am not mistaken, then why is it that you are not horsed and armoured as a knight Alured?" the knight asked.
" Sire I am the youngest of three sons and as such I am expected to make my own way in the world and make my fortune through my own efforts."
"Rest assured my brave young friend, you will find me a very grateful sponsor," the knight responded.

That night when they reached the camp of the besieging crusader army outside the walled city of Acre, Alured was treated as an honoured guest in the pavilion of Roger De Montgomery. He feasted with the Duke and his drinking vessel was topped up with strong wine from the best vineyards of Sicily all night. In the morning Alured regretted drinking quite so much and vowed to stick to ale in future.

The following day, the Duke and Alured rested from their exertions and conversed of many things, particularly of home. There were many preparations going on amongst Roger's retinue and Roger informed him that evening the King was to dine in his pavilion. Furthermore, Roger insisted that he would introduce his brave defender to the Lionheart.
"I shall see to it that your courage shall not go unrecognised in the highest places," vowed Earl Roger.
And so it was that Alured met his King and that when the King heard of Alured's brave deeds he made him kneel before him and knighted him that very evening.

During the siege of Acre, Alured spent many days fighting at the side of Roger De Montgomery and they took many spoils and prisoners when the siege was finally over.

When The Lionheart lost patience during negotiations with Saladin, he cruelly put many Saracen prisoners to the sword, but Alured had found favour with the King and managed to spare his prisoners, who were captained by a Saracen tribesman called Hakim. When Hakim saw the fate of the Saracens who were executed, he swore his allegiance to Alured. Without Alured's intervention, Hakim and his men would surely have met a cruel and untimely death.

In the days that followed, Hakim rendered Alured faithful service and the knight began to respect and admire him. In fact the sentiments were mutual. The respect for Hakim became widespread amongst the Crusaders and Roger De Montgomery himself, recognised Hakim as a man of honour.

When it became obvious that the Crusade was coming to an end and that the Crusaders were not going to win back Jerusalem from the hands of Saladin, Alured decided that he would give Hakim his freedom. However Hakim informed Alured that he had not yet satisfied his debt of honour and would be accompanying Alured back to England to continue in his service, until such time that the debt was repaid in full. Secretly Alured was glad that Hakim would travel with him and resolved that he would raise Hakim to a trusted position in his retinue, when they reached Staffordshire.

Soon after this Saladin and Richard Coeur de Leon reached a truce which allowed Christian pilgrims access to the city and in particular to Bethlehem which as the birthplace of Christ was the chosen destination of many pilgrims.

But always in the quiet house I heard,

Clear as a lark, high o'er me as a lark'

A sweet voice singing in the topmost tower

To the eastward: up I climbed a thousand steps

With pain: as in a dream I seemed to climb

Forever: at last I reached a door

A light was in the crannies, and I heard,

Glory and joy and honour to our Lord

And to the Holy Vessel of the Grail

Then in my madness I assayed the door;

It gave; and thru' a stormy glare, a heat

As from seven-times-heated furnace, I,

Blasted and burnt, and blinded as I was,

With such fierceness that I swooned away-

O, yet methought I saw the Holy Grail,

All palled in crimson samite, and around

Great angels, awful shapes, and wings and eyes.

Alfred, Lord Tennyson 'The Holy Grail'

Richard de Hastings, the Master of the Knights Templar, led the Saracen Hakim into a dark ante chamber dimly lit by the flames from a flickering torch. Making sure that the heavy cedar wood door of the chamber was firmly closed so they could not be overheard, and bolted so that they would not be disturbed, he began.

"Hakim though you are a Saracen, your courage and honour is well known to us. We know that you serve an English Knight called Alured Fitz Ormius. It is rumoured that you are to accompany this knight back to England?"

"It is true Sire that I have sworn an oath to serve Alured, since he mercifully spared my life at the siege of Acre, when many of my brothers perished at the hands of Coeur De Leon's executioners," replied Hakim.

"So it is true you are to return to the kingdom of England with your master, to continue in your service to him?"

"Indeed Sire it is. I am bound in honour to serve him for as long as he shall see fit, I owe him my life."

"Very well you have proved to be a most honourable and loyal man and as such the Knights Templar have an important task we wish you to undertake on our behalf. If you are willing to venture on this quest, we must ask you to swear a solemn oath. We cannot ask a Christian Knight, for fear that the secret may be revealed to the Church of Rome. This is why we have chosen to ask you, Hakim," Richard informed him.

"There are evil forces abroad that go about their business under cover of being Hospitalers. They seek that which we are entrusting to you. They will stop at nothing to recover it and return it to Pope Celestine. Those that wear the Black Teutonic Cross on their tabard must not be trusted"

"I understand Sire, but what is the task you require of me?"

"A simple matter of transporting a small object, a drinking vessel, to England and secreting it safely, in a place only known to you. No one will suspect that a Saracen carries a Holy Christian Relic," added Richard.

"This seems a simple task my Lord and well within my power."

"It may not be as simple as it sounds Hakim, there will be more danger attached to this quest than you imagine."

"Sire I can only promise to do my best."

"Very well," observed the Master, "make no mistake, you must not even mention this to Alured Fitz Ormius, as he has sworn his allegiance to Richard Coeur de Leon and he is a devout Christian Knight who would find it hard to keep this secret. Alured is a brave and honoured Knight, proven in battle, but his one weakness, which makes him unsuitable for our task, lies in his devout belief. Now you must swear a solemn oath that you will endeavour diligently to complete this quest."

"As Allah is my witness, I swear I will be faithful to this quest Sire."

Richard gave Hakim a plain wooden chalice, stained with age but wrapped in a rich silken cloth.

"This simple chalice is a Holy relic of no significance to a man of your beliefs, but one of great importance to our Order. Protect it with your life and trust no man, as it is a prize without equal in the whole of Christendom. You and your issue are henceforth chosen, to be the guardians of the greatest mystery of Christianity. There are those from Rome who seek the chalice for their own glorification and it must not fall into their hands. May God go with you and protect you from all dangers on your perilous journey across the sea to Cyprus and beyond, through the Holy Roman Empire and the Kingdom of France."

Richard unbolted the door to the chamber and took Hakim out through a side entrance into a quiet alley behind the Templar headquarters.

"Asalam alaykum," chanted Hakim.

"And peace be upon you too," responded the Master, as Hakim departed.

The Master wished Hakim success with all his heart. He knew that the Templars had chosen well and wistfully thought back to the days when he had been young and strong and wished that he had been honoured with a quest as important as the one they had chosen to give the Saracen.

Richard De Hastings was an old knight, the veteran of many battles with the scars to prove it. He believed he would never see his homeland again and hoped that Hakim's success and the small part he had played in it would stand him in good stead when the day came to meet his Maker.

Hakim was tall and straight limbed, lithe of movement, with speed and agility which belied his power.

He was a natural warrior, but more than this, he was a man of strong belief and honour. The Knights Templar had indeed chosen the right man to complete their mission.

The next months were taken up by the long and dangerous journey back to England. Dangerous, because it was well known that powerful men, who were not truly chivalrous knights, would capture returning crusaders and hold them to ransom, demanding that their families pay for their safe return. This foul practice went against the code of chivalry. Amongst other things, Knights swore they would protect the weak, be courteous, truthful and brave.

Indeed, this very event even befell the King of England, Richard the Lionheart himself. He was captured by King Leopold of Austria and was not released until a sum equal to three tons of silver was paid.

Alured and Hakim became firm friends on the long road back to England, assisting each other through the hardships of the arduous journey. Hakim disposed of the silken cloth which protected the vessel, as he thought it too unlikely that an old wooden chalice would be protected by such a rich covering. He did not want to arouse suspicion; he had been warned by the old Templar to observe the greatest caution.

Alured had managed to cover himself with glory during the short campaign and although the Crusaders had not achieved the goal of freeing Jerusalem many of them had grown rich from the spoils of war and Alured had done well selling the horses, weapons and armour he had captured to a wealthy Arab merchant before his departure from Acre.

But Alured's greatest achievement was to be rewarded by the patronage of Roger de Montgomery who gave him title to land in north Staffordshire as a reward for saving his life.

No-one who is in prison sees his fate
With honesty; for all he feels is sad -
But he can still compose a hopeful song.
I am so rich in friends, but poor in help:
They should be ashamed if, for my ransom,
I lie here one more year.

They know this all too well, my home, my lords,
The English, Norman, Poitevin, Gascon:
I never had a friend who was so poor
That I would leave them in their prison cell.
I do not sing these words to criticise –
Yet I am still in prison here.

Richard I written in captivity, summer 1193

6th Chapter
The Teutonic Knight Hospitallers

In Acre at the Hospice of Saint Mary, headquarters of the Teutonic Knight Hospitallers a very different briefing was taking place. Grand Master Gerhard who was charged by The Duke of Barbarossa with ensuring that Germanic Knights were given board and lodging when arriving in the Holy Land was briefing three obedient members of a secret Chapter of the Order. This secret Chapter was financed by Pope Celestine III and the reason for its existence was the quest for the Grail.

The three Germanic Knights, Konrad, Berghard, and Jorgen had been summoned with all haste to headquarters after Grand Master Gerhard had received some distressing news.

"My faithful knights," began the duplicitous Gerhard, "I have a mission of significance for you to carry out. It has come to our notice through information given by a reliable source that one Albert de Louvain is in league with the Knights Templar and has knowledge which is of the greatest importance to our quest. Unfortunately this news was received after his departure for France. It is believed that he will travel to Reims where he will be honoured by the Cardinals to become Bishop of Liege. You must follow him to France and obtain the information we desire. He may well be the courier of the Holy relic Pope Celestine is so anxious to recover. If not he will know where you must search.

When you have recovered either the relic or the information, he must be silenced for ever so that his knowledge cannot be passed on to the Templar's."

"Sire who is this Albert de Louvain?" asked Konrad.

He is the younger brother of the Abbot of a monastery in England run by the Cistercian Order at a place called Hultone. It is a rich and important monastery and the Abbot has many friends and much influence in Rome. So much so that his younger brother Albert is destined for high office in the Holy Roman Church. If he lives!" Gerhard laughed cruelly. "If you do not find him in Reims there is little doubt that he will be sheltered by his brother at Hultone Abbey."

"But Sire where is this Hultone?" requested Jorgen.

"It can be found in Staffordshire in the wastelands created by The Conqueror when the Saxon dogs would not come to heel." Gerhard sneered. "Now make all haste and do not forget to whom you owe allegiance and who pays your wages."

The three assassins left that very night to carry out their evil assignment. They followed the route of many a returning Crusader by ship to Malta and from there to Italy and through the Alps to France.

Once in France they took off the garb of the Teutonic knights and wore the tabards with the device of a Red Cross hoping that this would disguise their evil intentions.

Eventually after many weeks on horseback, saddle sore and weary they entered the city of Reims in north eastern France, they passed through the fortified walls and made straight for the Cathedral precincts. Once there they gained lodgings in a tavern and sought information about Albert de Louvain.

After plying the locals with strong ale they discovered that Albert was indeed to be found at Reims Cathedral where he was to be ordained as Bishop of Liege by Cardinal Guillaume aux Blanches Mains, Archbishop of Reims.

The next morning still wearing the disguise of the Red Cross they ventured to the Cathedral to seek Albert. He was found lying prostrate before the High Altar of the Cathedral carrying out his devotions. The knights waited patiently while Alfred completed his prayers and when he walked down the main aisle towards the Cathedral doors Konrad approached him.
"Forgive me Sire I seek out one Albert de Louvain with an important message from one in the Holy Land."
Albert looked startled at this and wondered if his secret alliance with the Knights Templar had led to this unexpected approach. Having been taught to be cautious he thought carefully before replying to this strange knight. "Sire I am indeed Albert but know not what you speak of and perhaps this is not the place to be having such a discourse?"
"Very well I understand your caution sire perhaps we should meet in a place less public?" Konrad replied.
The priest lowered his voice. "I take the morning air on horseback in the forest to the east of here. There is a bridge over the river which is easy to find. Perhaps we should talk further tomorrow?"
"Very well priest on the morrow it shall be and I will deliver my message then."
Konrad allowed Albert to leave the Cathedral before he and his accomplices retired to the tavern to make their plans and set their ambush for the morning.

Albert on returning to his cell thought long and hard about the knight he had met in the Cathedral that morning. All too aware that the knowledge he held could be dangerous to the cause of the Templars he decided that his best course of action was to send a coded message to his elder brother the Abbot of Hultone. He told him to warn Hakim that a strange knight had singled him out with the promise of a message from the Holy Land. If it was true the message could only be from Richard de Hastings the Master of the Knights Templar. However if it was false could only mean that the Teutonic Knights were on their trail.

He dispatched a trusted servant on a fast horse to deliver his message with all haste to England that very afternoon.

7ᵗʰ Chapter
The Knights Hospitaller Kill Albert de Louvain. November 1192.

Under cover of darkness, the following morning the three knights left the tavern. Knowing they would not return they had paid their dues the previous night. They knew that once they had dealt with Albert there would be no going back.

Reaching the bridge in the forest a little after dawn they set their trap. Konrad sat astride his charger in the middle of the bridge and Berghard and Jorgen concealed themselves in the thick undergrowth on the track leading to the bridge. This would enable them to follow up behind Albert and prevent his retreat.

In due course Albert passed by their hiding place with no suspicion of their presence and rode onto the wooden bridge to speak to Konrad.
"Hail Sir Knight," he greeted Konrad, "what is the message you carry from the Holy Land? It must be of great import for you have ridden so far to deliver it?"
"It is indeed good Priest and if you would approach a little closer I will tell you but I fear that even the trees may have ears."

As the priest came close Konrad drew a cudgel he was concealing ready to use from under his tabard and gave Alfred an almighty clout across his head which knocked him clean out of the saddle and left his brains addled. Meanwhile Jorgen and Berghard rode and helped Konrad tie his hands and sling him over his saddle, leading his horse deep into the woods where there would be no witness to their evil deeds.

They found a small clearing and tied the semi-conscious priest to a tree.
Whilst they waited for the priest to recover his wits Berghard lit a small fire and began to heat up the tip of his dagger. Berghard was the elected torturer and being a cruel man by nature he was hoping that the priest would resist his torture so that he could relish it the more.
When at last the priest opened his eyes Konrad splashed cold water from the stream in his face to bring him around a little faster.
"Who are you?" the priest weakly mumbled.
"That does not concern you. What does concern you is if you decide to give us that which we seek we will offer a quick and merciful release from this world. If however you decide to be awkward and delay us my friend Berghard here is particularly skilled in the art of torture and also has a liking for the task and I can guarantee you will not resist his ministrations. Before you die you will endure many hours of pain."
"Of what do you speak evil one?"
"I speak of the relic you have in your possession which is the rightful property of the Holy Roman Church."
"Relic? I have no relic."
Konrad nodded to Berghard who removing the dagger from the fire held the red hot tip close to Albert's eye before ripping his habit open and applying the tip to Albert's nipple.
The searing agony made Albert cry out for God but did not tempt him to give away his secret.
The torture and questioning went on long into the afternoon, until Konrad had revived the unfortunate priest many times with splashes of mercifully cool water to his skin.

Each time the priest refused to talk Berghard warmed to his task and thought of more places on Albert's body to apply the red hot dagger and elicit more pain and screams of agony.

Eventually after Berghard had extinguished one of Albert's eyes with the dagger at last he could stand no more. He still had sufficient courage to not tell all he knew but hoped he could tell them enough to satisfy them so that they would bring his life to a swift end and be on their way.

"The Grail which you seek is now far away," he groaned.

"Where is it Priest?" Konrad demanded.

"I know not. **Argghh**!!!!!!!!!!!" The priest screamed again as the red hot steel was applied to the inside of his ear down as far as his ear drum.

Konrad lifted Albert's head up by his hair. "Where exactly? I will have you tell me"

"To England, with a Saracen that's all I know."

Those were the last words the brave Albert ever spoke as Konrad drew his sword and rammed it into the priest's stomach and viciously twisted the blade before withdrawing it. Making sure that he would not be found alive Berghard used the pommel of his sword to cave in the priest's skull.

Then the three Teutonic Knights rode with all haste north to Calais to find a passage for England.

8ᵗʰ Chapter

North Staffordshire Spring 1193

Alured and Hakim breasted the rise at Chell and whilst they rested their horses for a while Alured pointed out the hills of Biddulph Moor to the Saracen.

"See yonder my faithful servant, this is the land inherited from my father. To the north are the hills, from whence spring the sweet waters of the River Trente, where you shall be my trusted Bailiff. Below to the dexter is the valley of Knypersley, where we shall build a great hall and make it our home. There is timber a plenty and rich pasture where we shall graze our beasts. As our fortunes prosper we can clear more woodland to create pasture. There is sweet water from the Trente which never fails in the driest of summers."

"Sire it is verdant pasture land with many trees, quite unlike my homeland. I am sure that by the grace of Allah and much hard work we will prosper."

"Prosper we shall my good man and when we have a decent roof over our heads and enough food for the longest hardest winter we shall have to find wives to bear us many strong children, both for myself and for you," teased Alured.

"My liege, I am but a humble servant and have not the means to support a wife and children."

"Trust me, you have served me well and I will show my gratitude, you shall be my Bailiff and first among my household and you shall have the wherewithal to support a wife and many children. There will be many a comely wench casts her eye in your direction," continued the Knight chuckling.

"My liege I shall be content to fulfil my obligations to you and have no desire to take to me a wife," protested the Saracen.

"We shall see, we shall see," the knight laughed, knowingly.

With peasants from his brothers estate at Darlastone Alured and Hakim soon built a sturdy hall on the hill overlooking Knypersley and warm huts for the peasants. They hunted enough boar and deer to see them through their first winter and planted oats and barley to provide them with enough to eat the following year. The weather was kind and due to their hard work they did indeed prosper.

Twelve months after their arrival in Knypersley a monk came to Alured with a message from the Abbot of Hultone Abbey. The monk told Alured and Hakim of the arrival of three strangers, Germanic Knights who were asking questions about a Saracen and an English Knight and that the Abbot had received a warning from his younger brother in Reims that these strangers were not to be trusted. Hakim listened closely to what the monk said and resolved that he would stick closely to Alured until all danger was passed. Alured told the monk to assure the Abbot that he would be cautious if the strangers showed up. Hakim decided that he would make sure his scimitar and his bow and quiver were with him at all times.

Sure enough a couple of days later the Knights who were scouring the area came upon Alured felling a tree.

Hakim was a little way off and was unobserved by the three Knights. One of the knights approached Alured and began a conversation. Hakim was just a little too distant to hear what was being said but took his arrows from his quiver and stuck them in the sward by his feet and put the bow string into the notch of one in readiness.

Suddenly without warning the three knights launched a vicious assault on Alured who being wary was quick enough to use the axe to protect himself before the blows came raining down upon him.

Hakim drew his bow and launched a bodkin arrow which took Konrad squarely between the shoulder blades pierced his chain mail and emerged through the front of his chest. The other two paused to look around and Alured seized his opportunity and neatly removed Jorgen's head with one almighty blow of his axe. Before the evil Berghard could react a second arrow from Hakim's bow pierced his ribs lifting him of his feet.

The Saracen had quickly followed this arrow and as the evil torturer lay gasping his last on the ground Hakim thrust his dagger through the knight's visor bursting his eyeball and entering his brain.

They found a secluded part of the woods above the Knypersley valley and buried the bodies of the three assassins after removing their armour and weapons which Alured took as spoils of battle and kept in the Great Hall. Hakim took the two riding mares and the packhorse on to Biddulph Moor and let them roam with the Arabian stallion he had brought with him from the Holy Land. The one remaining stallion Alured took as a gift for his brother Robert.

Alured had no idea why he had been attacked and he questioned Hakim closely.

"Why do you suppose three Knights far from home should turn up here and attack me Hakim?"

"I know not sire but 'twas lucky for us that the monk brought us a warning."

"By the garb we found on their pack horse they were obviously Knight Hospitaller's and they are a very secret chapter, some believe they are under direct command of the Papacy."

"If that is true sire then maybe it has something to do with the ransom being demanded for the return of Richard Coeur de Leon? They say he is prisoner of Leopold Duke of Austria, and he is reputed to be a strong ally of the Pope," replied Hakim.

"It is a well known fact that the Pope was sorely aggrieved when King Richard gave the island of Cyprus to the Knights Templar. Perhaps it has something to do with that," concluded Alured.

Hakim nearly confessed everything but remembering his oath to Richard de Hastings he kept his own counsel but decided that he must find somewhere permanent to hide the Grail.

Over the period of the next few years the pair did indeed grow prosperous. The knight went in search to Hampshire and discovered Catherine still unmarried and living in a village close to the small wool town called Andeferas, now called Andover. During the intervening years Catherine had stoutly resisted all suitors in the hope that one day Alured would come in search of her. He asked Catherine's brother for her hand in marriage. He gave his consent gladly and they were married in the church of St Mary, Andover. Then Alured returned to Knypersley with his new bride. They were very happy together and she gave him a fine son to continue the line and two daughters. They worked hard and treated the serfs fairly and the estate grew prosperous. The corn grew thick, the cattle fat and there was excellent hunting in the hills around. There was never an empty belly in Knypersley.

Eventually the two lovers were laid to rest together in the aisle of Burton Abbey their shared tomb stone bearing witness to their true and lasting love for one another.

As predicted by Alured, many rosy cheeked lass cast her eye in the Saracen's direction, but he seemed immune to all their charms. Truthfully, the quest he had been given by the Templars, was weighing heavily upon him, for he had not found a suitable hiding place for the humble wooden chalice entrusted to him. He had to be certain that wherever he concealed the vessel, that it would be suitably protected.

As was the custom of those times, Alured and the rest of his entourage, entertained each other during the long winter evenings, with stories and poems, passed down from generation to generation.

They all enjoyed Alured's stories of the Holy Land and were fascinated by Hakim's accounts of his life in Syria and service in the army of Saladin. Then one evening Hakim found the answer, to the problem which was troubling him sorely.

Alured recounted the legend of Alderley Edge and how since the time of the legendary king Arthur, one hundred knights in their armour and their one hundred milk white steeds lay asleep in a secret cave under the ground, ready to defend England in her hour of need. Hakim listened intently to the tale and later that night could not sleep with excitement, thinking that a secret cave protected by one hundred knights, would be an ideal place for him to hide the wooden chalice.

The next day Hakim casually enquired where Alderley was and was pleased to learn that it was only a half days ride to the north of Knypersley. He resolved that he would go in search of the hidden cave and take the chalice with him, as soon as he could excuse his absence.

Hakim often spent time alone on Biddulph Moor, hunting wolves and tending the land that Alured had given him for his own. So he knew that he would not be missed in Knypersley, if he went in search of the cave.

BIDDULPH MOOR

9th Chapter

Encounter at Alderley.

Mighty the Wizard
Who found me at sunrise
Sleeping, and woke me
And learn'd me Magic!
Great the Master,
And sweet the Magic,

Alfred, Lord Tennyson 'Merlin and The Gleam'

The opportunity for Hakim to explore Alderley Edge, arose sooner than he had expected, as Alured was called away to Stafford to attend on Duke Robert II, at Stafford castle.

After Alured left, Hakim retrieved the chalice from its temporary hiding place in his lodge at Biddulph, saddled his horse and set off without delay, eager to try and conclude his quest.

He paused at the end of Biddulph Moor, on an escarpment called The Cloud, where all of Cheshire was spread before him.

The view from CLOUD

After several hours hard riding he arrived at Alderley Edge.

The path leading to the top of the Edge was steep and thickly wooded and Hakim soon found it necessary to dismount and proceed on foot. Presently, he reached the top and exploring through the woodland, came upon a clearing. There was an oddly shaped rock sticking up from the ground.

Hakim sat on the rock to regain his breath and was just about to stand and continue his search for the entrance to the cave when an old man becloaked and leaning heavily on a strangely twisted staff, appeared through the trees and approached the place where Hakim rested.

"Good morrow traveller, you are far from home," the old man addressed Hakim.

"Good morrow old man, 'tis not that far from Biddulph Moor."

"I speak of the land far to the East from which you have journeyed. I have the honour of addressing Hakim the Saracen, do I not?" enquired the old man.

Hakim taken by great surprise by this question grew instantly suspicious and asked, "Have we met before old man?"

"Indeed young man, we have never met, but your reputation precedes you sir and besides I know many things which mere mortals do not," replied the old man mysteriously.

"Do you talk to me in riddles old man?" demanded Hakim

"I know the answers to many riddles and I know why you are here. Have you brought that which you were entrusted to deliver?"

"Why would it be of interest to you old man?"

"I will show you why if you follow me," said the old man. With that he struck the rock where Hakim had been sitting with his twisted staff and there was an enormous CRACK and a fissure opened up in the rock revealing a set of iron gates.

"Come with me and I will show you what you seek," said the old man pushing the gates apart with his strange staff.

Hakim followed the old man into the cave and when his eyes grew used to the dim light, he realised when he spied the rows of sleeping Knights and their milk white steeds, his quest was finally at an end.

"These are the Knights of the Brotherhood of the Round Table and I am Merlin the wizard, entrusted with the secret of Alderley for all time. One day, when England is in dire peril these valiant knights will arise from their slumber and defend the realm from its enemies. This is the place where you shall leave the vessel which you have carried from the Holy Land. From this day forth these knights will take the responsibility of protecting the Grail. And you and your issue shall protect the secret of the resting place, revealing it to no man. In return for the Grail, I will give you this silver unicorn and promise you that if you are ever in danger grasp it tightly and say these words, "Allh ysaadny" and the magic of the unicorn shall be your protector."

The wizard passed Hakim a silver medallion embossed with a unicorn hanging from a silver chain.

"Sire, I don't pretend to understand all that I have seen here today, but I swore an oath and my honour forbids me to break it. Your secret will be safe with me," promised Hakim.

"Now follow me out into the sun Hakim, for from this day forth the sun will forever shine on you and yours," said Merlin.

The wizard led Hakim from the cave, giving him great riches along the way from the precious jewels and gold coinage collected there.

When they arrived outside in the weak winter sunlight, the old man walked away, leaning heavily on his staff and disappeared into the trees. When Hakim turned around, the entrance to the cave had vanished.

Hakim returned to the bottom of the wooded slope where he had left his mount and tired but elated ,with a sense of satisfaction that his duty had been done, returned back to Biddulph Moor where he spend the night in his lodge. The following morning he was back at the great hall in Knypersley, before his master returned from Stafford Castle.

In the many years that followed, Alured and Hakim did indeed prosper and the sun always seemed to shine on Hakim. Eventually now that he was more at peace with himself, Hakim took a wife, a comely auburn haired lass, with straight limbs and a willing smile. Together they had six sons and three daughters.

The dynasty of "The Dark Men of Biddulph" was founded by the Saracens genes and to this day swarthy men with the surname Bailey can still be found in North Staffordshire.

In the twilight of his years great sadness overcame the old Saracen, when his wife died and he began to hanker for the land of his birth.

Alured had died many years since and on his deathbed had made Hakim a freeman.

Hakim decided to undertake the long journey back to Syria and after many adventures and always protected by the silver unicorn he at last reached the oasis of his brother. He discovered that although his brother was also dead, his son, Hakim's nephew, welcomed him with great celebrations.

Hakim and his nephew became very fond of each other and spent many hours talking and discussing matters of family and honour. Hakim soon respected his nephew as a devout man of his word and trusted him as he would his own sons.

Hakim grew ill and realised that his frail body would never allow the journey back to England. Instead of passing on the silver unicorn to his eldest son, he would have to give it and the secret of Alderley Edge to his nephew.

That evening he told his nephew the full story, gave him the silver medallion and made him memorise the phrase "Allh ysaadny"

Sometime during that night, Hakim died peacefully in his sleep. The issue he sired on Biddulph Moor lives on through his bloodline, as evidenced by the appearance of the "Dark Men of Biddulph Moor" to this day. There is still a hill on the Moor called Bailey's Hill which reminds us the land once belonged to the Bailiff of the Manor, Hakim the Saracen.

10th Chapter

Monday morning Macclesfield 2010

Shariff was on his way to school. He had done his chores, making sure that his brothers had their breakfast and had done the washing up, whilst his busy mother, opened up the shop for the early morning customers. His father had left the house at 6.30 that morning, heading for Wilmslow, hoping to pick up some early morning business for his taxi. His father worked long unsociable hours and Shariff rarely saw him apart from when they visited the mosque to pray.

Shariff was hoping he wouldn't run into Wayne Piggot and his band of thugs that morning. They had been making Shariff's life difficult for weeks, twisting his arm and forcing him to give them his dinner money. This was the reason why Shariff had asked his mother if he could take a packed lunch instead. They often spat on him and they mocked and ridiculed him at every opportunity.

It wasn't that Shariff was scared of them; it was just that he hoped they would eventually tire of their bullying and leave him alone. Besides he had his unicorn for protection and had been told that if he was ever in real danger, the silver medallion would protect him. Well, that was the the story anyhow. That was what his uncle Hussein had told him, when he had given Shariff the medallion and made Hakim memorise the phrase "Allh ysaadny" before his family had left Damascus for England. Hussein had told him that the unicorn was very old and had originally come from England close to where Shariff was going to live.

This morning he was out of luck. The gang of three were hiding in the bushes in the park waiting for him to pass so they could ambush him. As he approached the bushes they jumped on him and Wayne Piggot bent his arm painfully up his back.

"Where ja fink yor goin then?" Wayne spat in his ear.

"Yeh where ya goin then?" echoed Micky and Frankie, who weren't really blessed with a great deal of imagination and often repeated what Wayne, the brains of the outfit, had already said like two trained parrots.

"Let go! I'm on my way to school, where do you think I'm going at this time on a Monday morning?" grimaced Sharrif hoping they wouldn't find the £3.50 he had in his pocket to pay for the school trip to Alderley Edge later that week.

"Wot 'ave yer got in yer bag then?" demanded Wayne.

"Yeh wot yer got in yer bag?" parroted Micky and Frankie.

Frankie wrenched the bag from Shariff's shoulder and scattered the contents on the wet grass. The Haloumi cheese sandwiches he had made that morning fell from his lunch box into the mud and the carton of apricot yoghurt split open as it was thrown violently against a tree trunk by Micky.

"Nufink 'ere Wayne," chanted Frankie.

"Ye he aint got nufink Wayne," echoed Micky.

"Wot yer got in yer pockets then Paki?" yelled Wayne and tripped Shariff onto his back and pinned his shoulders down into the wet grass, with his knees.

Shariff struggled hard but Wayne was too strong and heavy to push off.

"Micky see worr'is gorr' in 'is pockets," ordered Wayne.

Micky assisted by Frankie turned out Shariff's pockets and soon found the envelope containing the school trip money.

"Give it us 'ere," said Wayne snatching it out of Micky's hand.

Ripping open the envelope Wayne found the three pound coins and the fifty pence Shariff had put in from his money box that morning.

"Free quid for me and fifty pence between you two," announced Wayne incapable of working out that meant twenty five pence apiece for his accomplices.

"And don't try 'oldin out on us again Paki scum," threatened Wayne as he pocketed his share.

As a parting shot, he kicked Shariff in the stomach and the other two spat on him and then they all ran off laughing and shouting, "Paki, Paki," until they were out of earshot.

"I'm not from Pakistan," he shouted after them. "I'm from Syria and can speak Arabic."

But it all fell on deaf ears.

When Shariff arrived at school, he was very dishevelled and very late. The Deputy Head Mr Burton signed him into the dreaded red late book and sent him to the boy's toilets, to try and scrape the mud from his clothes and hands.

When Shariff finally arrived in his classroom, Miss Steele had already started the numeracy lesson. It didn't worry Shariff as he was good at maths, another reason why he wasn't popular with Wayne and his gang.

Miss Steele looked at him sympathetically and continued her exposition to the class. It wasn't until later, that she found the time to enquire why he had mud stains on his trousers.

"I just fell over in the park on my way to school," explained Shariff. Miss Steele was a young teacher, but she was perceptive and secretly she doubted that this was the complete story. However, she realised that Shariff didn't want to make a fuss and reluctantly let the matter drop. She suspected that Shariff was getting a hard time from some of the rougher boys in the class and was hoping that eventually he would confide in her.

When it came to collecting the money for the trip to Alderley Edge, Shariff told her he had forgotten it and that he would bring it the next day.

Shariff didn't have any real friends in the class except for a girl called Rani, who had taken a shine to him when his family had arrived in Macclesfield from Damascus. She was drawn towards him because she too had been the subject of teasing from the other girls and so knew what he was suffering.

At lunch time she found him out, in a corner of the yard.

"Had some trouble with Wayne and his gang this morning?" she enquired.

"Yes," admitted Shariff.

"What did they do?"

"They stole my trip money and ruined my sandwiches and spilt my yoghurt," he told her.

"Never mind, I have plenty of sandwiches, you can share mine, but you should tell Miss you know," she advised.

"Yes I know, but if I do it will cause more trouble and she won't be able to stop them getting me on my way home or in the mornings on my way to school."

"You should tell, Miss would sort it out, she's kind and very clever," said Rani who was Miss Steele's biggest fan, along with Mr Burton the Deputy Head. All the kids had noticed he was sweet on Miss

Steele. He was always blushing when she was around and some of the older girls were saying he should ask her out, but he was obviously having trouble plucking up courage. Some of the older boys said that their dads fancied her and anyway, she was well out of Mr Burton's league.

Rani didn't listen, 'cos she thought that Mr Burton was nice too and that they would make a lovely couple, he was always helping Miss and he had even volunteered to drive the school minibus to Alderley Edge, later that week. Even at a tender age Rani could recognise true lve when she saw it.

Rani had always wanted to be a bridesmaid and had secret dreams that if they ever got married, she might be asked by Miss to walk down the aisle holding the train of a beautiful white wedding dress. Rani liked the colourful celebrations of a typical Hindu wedding but really loved the traditional English bridal gown.

As Shariff hurried home that night he was hoping he could put his trousers and shirt in the washer, before his mother noticed how muddy they were.

He opened the shop door and of course the bell gave him away. His mother, thinking a customer had come into the shop saw immediately the mess Shariff's clothes were in.

"Shariff, what a mess! How did you get into such a state?" she demanded.

"Sorry mother," apologised Shariff who was always respectful of his parents knowing how hard they both worked. Coming to England was a great wrench for his mother to be away from relatives left behind in Damascus but it meant a chance for the family to better themselves away from the political strife of the military dictatorship.

"Well go upstairs immediately and get changed then you can watch your brothers for me while you do your homework," said Mum who was always glad for the help Shariff gave her with his two little brothers when he returned home from school.

Shariff went upstairs and took off his muddy trousers and put them in the washing basket in the bathroom. Then he found his Port Vale shirt and a pair of jeans and was ready to start his homework.

First he read a chapter of his reading book called "The BFG" which was a very funny story. Then he finished off the maths sheet he had missed out because he was late for school. It didn't take him long it was only decimal fractions and he was good at that.

Then he played with his little brothers until it was time for tea. He wondered what time his father would return and if he would take him to watch the Vale play Crewe on Saturday. It was a local derby and should be a good game. Meanwhile he had the school trip to look forward to, if only he could keep out of Wayne's way.

Perhaps he should take Rani's advice and tell Miss Steele. The only trouble was Miss Steele wouldn't be able to walk him home every night and she wouldn't be around at weekends either!

The following morning Sharrif completed his usual chores helping his mother to dress and feed his brothers their breakfast. Making sure he had everything ne needed for school in his bag he set off. Deciding to take a longer more roundabout route Sharrif was successful in avoiding the attentions of Wayne and his snot nosed followers.

Today was swimming and Sharrif had his trunks and towel in his bag.
The first part of the morning passed without incident registration was followed by numeracy which Sharrif enjoyed. Then came morning break when it all went wrong.

Sharrif entered the cloakroom and was looking in his bag hanging on his peg for the biscuits he had wrapped in cling film that morning he was seized and his arms pinned from behind.
"Wot yer got in the bag Paki?" asked the unmistakeable voice of Wayne.
"Nothing that would interest you"
"Oh yeh I'll be the judge of that."
"Yeh we'll be the judge of that!" echoed the voices of Micky and Frankie.
Wayne took Sharrif's bag from the peg and tipped the contents upside down onto the cloakroom floor. The other kids in the class had made themselves scarce, they knew better than to tangle with Wayne.

Seeing the biscuits Wayne stamped on them and crushed hi boot down and ground them into the cloakroom floor. Luckily he ignored Shariff's lunch box. Then finding nothing else of interest in the contents he picked up the towel and told his mates to follow him into the boy's toilets. While Micky and Frankie held Sharrif Wayne took great delight in stuffing Sharrif's towel into the porcelain trough of the urinal.
"There ya go Paki a nice towel covered in piss for your trip to the baths this morning. You stink of curry anyway so it'll make no difference to you." Wayne sniggered.
"Come on you pair we ain't got all day ya know we'd better get out onto that yard before old Burton catches us in 'ere."

After they left Sharrif did his best to wash the towel in a hand basin but of course it was no use it did smell and there was no way he could use it at the swimming baths.
When the class lined up after break Sharrif had to tell Miss Steele that he had forgotten to bring a towel. She sent him to spend the rest of the morning with Mr Burton in his class room.
Of course Wayne and Micky and Frankie were there too as they had been banned from swimming lessons for bad behaviour on the bus. For the rest of the morning Shariff had to put up with their stupid grins, face pulling and sly taunts.

When the bell went for lunch Sharrif hung around to help Mr Burton tidy up to give time for Wayne and Co to disappear.
"Not like you to forget your kit Sharrif." began Mr Burton.
"No Sir."
"Are you having some sort of problem at home?"
"No Sir."
"You enjoy swimming lessons don't you?"

"Yes Sir"

"Then I suggest you buck your ideas up in future."

"Yes Sir."

"Run along then and get your lunch now."

"Yes Sir."

Sharrif made his way to the dining hall hoping that he wouldn't run into Wayne.

Sharrif ate his lunch with Rani who had returned from the swimming baths.

"What happened to you?" she asked him.

"Wayne stuffed my towel down the toilet and it was soaked so I told Miss I'd forgotten it."

"You really should tell someone about this, you know."

"I don't think that would stop them, I 'm hoping they will get bored and find someone else to pick on."

"That's a bit of a selfish attitude isn't it?"

"I suppose so but I really don't think that telling anyone at school will help."

"I think you'd be surprised. Bullies are usually cowards too. If Mr Burton got onto their case or even Mrs Herbert they'd soon be sorry."

Mrs Herbert was the headmistress and although she was kind she didn't tolerate any sort of misbehaviour.

"Maybe?" was all that Sharrif could say in reply he didn't like to disagree with Rani but still thought his way of dealing with things was best.

The afternoon passed without event and Sharrif made his way home by yet another circuitous route to avoid Wayne and his gang.

His mother was busy in the shop and Sharrif went straight into the kitchen to put his smelly towel into the washing machine before his mother discovered the state that it was in.

Once he had done that he played with his brothers and tried to do his Literacy homework.

Once the shop had closed for the evening and the brothers were in bed Sharrif's mother asked him how swimming had gone that day. Sharrif told her that it was fine and that soon he would get his length certificate.

Sharrif went to bed with a heavy heart that night as he lay awake trying to find a solution to the problems which were beginning to make him feel very miserable .Nothing came to mind and he eventually fell asleep clutching the Unicorn pendant tightly in his hand.

12th Chapter

Wednesday

Sharrif woke late to hear his mother calling him to get up for breakfast. He hurriedly showered and dressed and raced downstairs to gobble down his muesli and pack his bag for school. His mother had prepared him some tortilla wraps with tomato, peppers and goats cheese the night before and she took them out of the refrigerator and made sure Sharrif put them in his bag. One last check to make sure he had his Literacy homework to hand in to Miss Steele and he hit the street at a run. He knew that being late was playing straight into the hands of Wayne. Wayne and his mates were not early risers being far too lazy to get up in time for school on far too many occasions. They had a record of late attendance.

Sharrif decided to take the most direct route to school through the park and hope that Wayne wasn't there lying in wait.

Unknown to Sharrif Wayne, Micky and Frankie were already in the park having decided that they were going to play truant for the day. Wayne had nicked a packet of cigarettes and a lighter from his mother and they were all three busy puffing away when they spotted Sharrif entering the park.

"Quick hide you pair. Here comes the Paki." hissed Wayne.

They all three hid in the rhododendron bushes and waited for Shariff to pass by.

As Sharrif drew level with their hiding place Wayne stuck out a boot and tripped him sending him sprawling onto the tarmac of the path. Wayne quickly jumped on Sharrif pinning his shoulders to the ground with his knees.

"Where you off to in such a rush Paki?"

"Where do you think school of course?"

Wayne had an idea to torment Shariff and dripped a gob of spit into Sharrif's face. Then continued to tease him by allowing drool to hang from his mouth over Sharrif's face, sometimes sucking back up into his mouth and sometimes letting it fall.

Sharrif struggled but could not escape the stronger boy.

Wayne's disgusting spit dribbled down Shariff's face

"Wa sup Paki don't yer like a wash in the morning then?" grinned Wayne. "Won't do yer any 'arm yer know I ain't got foot and mouth or anyfink"

Micky and Frankie thought this humiliation of Sharrif was hilarious and goaded Wayne on.

"Yeh go on Wayne show 'im what a bit of English Spit tastes like. Better than all that stinkin' curry he eats!"

Once again the two grabbed Shariff's bag and emptied it onto the path. Disappointed not to discover any money they found his lunchbox.

"What's this foreign muck in 'ere then?" demanded Micky.

"Give us a look." ordered Wayne getting up off Sharrif and painfully lifting him of the ground by twisting his arm.

"Looks like he brought some stuff to feed the ducks," Wayne suggested. "C'mon Paki let's go an feed the ducks."

Wayne dragged Sharrif over to the duck pond and handed him the lunchbox.

"Now then Paki feed them ducks." He ordered.

Wayne and the gang were not satisfied until they had made Shariff throw all his lunch to the ducks.

Then for good measure when it was all gone Wayne took the plastic box and launched it far out into the lake where it bobbed about for a while before it sank.

"Aww look it's gone for a lickle swim. Go on then fetch it Paki!" with that Wayne gave Sharrif an almighty push and he went face first into the pond.

When Sharrif surfaced and climbed out of the pond soaking wet he was shaking with anger as much as cold. The three bullies were away on the far side of the park chanting "Paki had a paddle, Paki had a paddle."

There was nothing for it now, Sharrif would have to go home and get changed.

When he returned to the shop his mother was shocked to see the state he was in.

"Goodness me Sharrif what have you being doing?"

"I took a shortcut to school and fell in the pond."

"Go straight upstairs and into the shower before you catch your death of cold."

Sharrif went up stairs, showered, put on some dry clothes and put his wet clothing into the washer.

When he had done all this it was almost time for lunch, so he made a cheese sandwich and a cup of tea for him and his mother and took it to her in the shop.

The shop was not busy so they ate their sandwich and drank their tea together.

"Sharrif you would tell me if you were in trouble of any kind wouldn't you" she asked.

"Yes mother don't worry."

"Good boy, I don't think you should go to school now. Take the afternoon off I want to keep my eye on you in case you get ill. There must be all sorts of horrible germs in that dirty old pond."

Sharrif was quite relieved that he wouldn't be facing Wayne who was the biggest most horrible germ he knew again that day and had a pleasant afternoon helping his mother, looking after his brothers while she minded the shop.

Dreaming the Unicorn

I dreamed I saw the Unicorn
Last night
It rippled through the forest,
pearly white
breathing a moonlight silence.

Its single horn
Stood shining like a lance
I saw it toss its head
and snort and prance
and paw the midnight air
Its mane was like a mass
of silver hair

But suddenly it shuddered
It sensed my spellbound gaze,
my wondering eyes
and turned to look upon me with surprise,
seeming to read my face
and looking as if to say
"You are not from this place.
What is your business here?"

My mind was far from clear.
I could not think or speak.
Above my head, I heard the branches creak
and then, from where I stood,
I watched it flicker off into the wood,
into the velvet space between the trees.

A sudden rush of rapid midnight breeze,
that felt both chill and deep,
awoke me from my sleep
and there upon the pillow by my head
I found a strand of shining silver thread.

I kept that strand of mane,
I keep it, still,
inside a box upon my window sill,
And when the world hangs heavy
on my brain
it helps me dream the unicorn again.

Tony Mitton

They had all eaten their evening meal and while his mother was busy in the shop he read his brothers a bedtime story, until they both fell asleep. His father still wasn't home. Shariff often worried about how tired his father looked from the long hours he worked.

As he was coming back down the stairs, he heard a man's voice shouting in the shop and then he was shocked to hear his mother scream.

Shariff jumped down the last four stairs and rushed through the living room and burst through the door into the shop.

Shariff saw three rough looking men and his mother was on the floor sobbing, while one of them shouted at her, demanding to know where the rest of the money was. Shariff could see that the till was already empty and that one of the men was filling a bag with cigarettes and other items from the shop which took his fancy. The third man was guarding the door. The man who was shouting moved towards the living room door and Shariff immediately thought of his brothers upstairs asleep. He flew at the big man who was shouting at his distressed mother. The man pushed him off violently and Shariff hit his head on the shop counter as he fell over. Lying there on the floor, stunned, he suddenly remembered the silver unicorn and clutching the pendant in his hand he repeated the phrase his uncle had taught him

"Allh ysaadny"

Immediately everything turned misty and appeared in slow motion. From out of nowhere appeared a shining white unicorn, which set about the three men with a vengeance, making them squeal with pain each time the unicorn stabbed them with its spiral horn or kicked them with its hooves. They were no match for the unicorn and in no time at all were madly scrambling to try and escape from the shop. They abandoned the bag and the money they had taken and were running away down the road with the unicorn in hot pursuit, when a police car turned the corner and two policemen chased and soon overpowered all three of them and had them handcuffed, with surprisingly little resistance.

Strangely, when they were later interviewed at the police station, none of the villains remembered the unicorn and had no explanation for the bruises all over their bodies.

One of the policemen had thought he had seen a white horse running down the road, but couldn't be sure that he wasn't imagining it.

Of course, the only one who knew for certain what had happened was Shariff and he was giving nothing away.

The following morning, Shariff did not go to school. As the shop was such a mess he stopped at home, to help his mother tidy up. That meant he was there when a reporter from the Sentinel arrived at the shop for an interview later that morning.

His mother told the reporter how horrible the three men were and how brave Shariff had been.

It turned out that the gang had been responsible for a string of robberies of off licences and shops all over Cheshire and the greater Manchester area.

That evening there was a front page article and a large photograph of Shariff in the newspaper, hailing him as a hero. He wanted to tell everyone that it was really the unicorn, but who would believe him? So he held his silence and told no one.

He did wonder about the unicorn and the magic which had been entrusted to him but there was no one who he could talk to about it.

He knew that the unicorn was very old and that it had passed down through many generations of his family in Damascus. He knew that a unicorn was supposed to be a mythical beast. He had learned from English lessons at school that mythical beasts didn't exist in reality but it had seemed real enough when it was stamping and kicking out at those robbers. He smiled when he recalled the shouts and squeals uttered by the robbers when the unicorn had set about them making them flee in a very short time. Always the way with cowards he knew that they should be confronted but that was not his way. He had seen much violence and unrest when his family lived in Syria and had no wish to become involved if it could possibly be avoided.

14th Chapter

Bullies Defeated

The following morning was Friday the day of the trip and Shariff had been looking forward to it for ages. He carefully hid his £3.50 in his shoe, so that if he was ambushed, Wayne wouldn't find it.

He arrived at school without incident and was quite surprised when the parents waiting around the school gate recognised him and gave him a big round of applause. They had all read the Sentinel and had recognised Shariff as the hero the article was written about. In any case most of the parents used Shariff's mother's corner shop and knew the family.

Shariff got quite a reception from the other children and lots of them made a fuss of him and said he was a hero.

In assembly that morning the headmistress Mrs Herbert read out the newspaper article to the children and showed them all the photograph of Shariff on the front page. The whole school gave him three cheers.

In class Miss Steele said that she hoped the hero hadn't forgotten his trip money and was surprised when Shariff retrieved it from his shoe and gave it to her.

"Shariff why on Earth was your trip money in your shoe?" asked Miss Steele

Before he knew what he was doing he replied "So that Wayne and his gang don't steal it Miss."

Then the whole story of the continual bullying and the incident of the towel came tumbling out and Wayne and Micky and Frankie were sent straight to Mrs Herbert the headmistress's office. Miss Steele told Shariff that he wasn't to worry any more as she was sure he wouldn't be bothered by Wayne again, not when the headmistress had finished with him.

The bullies were still missing when the rest of the class was getting on the minibus and so they left for Alderley Edge without them.

Mr Burton seemed very happy and made some jokes about Shariff being Macclesfield's answer to Superman and they all laughed and Miss Steele smiled and laughed at all of Mr Burton's jokes, no matter how corny they were. Mr Burton also blushed a lot.

Shariff felt better now that he had got everything off his chest and wondered why he hadn't told Miss Steele about the bullies before. He was now feeling a lot more confident and beginning to think that maybe he might find some friends in his class after all. They were all keen to speak to him and to listen to what he had to say and lots of them offered him a sweet and wanted to be his partner for the nature walk on Alderley Edge. But Shariff knew who he was going to choose to be his partner, Rani of course.

The journey from Macclesfield to Alderley Edge is only a short one by road and they soon arrived in the car park of the Wizard Inn.

Waiting for them in the car park was the landlord of the Inn, Mr Garnet. He was a Cheshire man born and bred and had lived in Alderley Edge all his life. His father had been a farmer at nearby Adderbank Farm and what Mr Garnet didn't know about the plants and animals which lived on the Edge wasn't worth knowing. He also knew the Legend of the Sleeping Knights and told the children the story as they climbed the path through the trees to the top.

Mr Garnet showed the children all the named spots on the Edge and told them all about Bronze Age men living on the Edge and about how mines were dug to retrieve copper and why copper was a valuable metal.

They stopped for lunch near to a place he called Stormy Point and Mr Garnet showed them the strange rock protruding from the earth. They sat and ate their sandwiches and everyone was keen to tell Mr Garnet what a hero Shariff was and he congratulated Shariff and said he thought he was very brave.

After lunch, they tidied up and made sure they left no litter and Mr Garnet said he was now going to show them the finest view in all Cheshire. As they walked along the path which led out of the clearing, Shariff thought he saw something moving through the trees, back where they had come from.

STORMY POINT ALDERLEY EDGE

Painted by the Author

15th Chapter

The Cave

Shariff turned around to watch the through the trees and suddenly, he was alone. The others had moved off and he had become detached from the rest of the party. Even Rani had not noticed he was missing.

He walked back towards Stormy Point. What was it he had seen? He was sure he had spotted a strange figure moving stealthily through the birch trees. He reached the rock and sat down and then noticed that there was a stooped figure approaching through the trees, leaning heavily on a strangely twisted staff. As the figure neared Shariff saw it was an old man, with long white hair and a beard, wearing a fur cloak. He sat perfectly still and although his mother had always instructed him to be cautious with strangers, he was not afraid.

"Greetings young Shariff," the old man saluted him "I have waited many years for you."

"What do you mean Sir? How do you know my name?" answered Shariff.

"The things I've seen and the knowledge I have gained whilst waiting for you would surprise you my friend. I am Merlin the Wizard who advised and protected King Arthur a thousand years ago and I have waited here for you, for over eight hundred years, since I met your ancestor Hakim the Saracen on this very spot in the year 1198."

"I'm not sure I know what you mean Sir," said Shariff. "I have never heard of an ancestor called Hakim."

" Well young Sire I know that you are a brave and honest boy who has borne his problems with stoicism and I also know that the silver unicorn brought you here, so that I may reward you and reveal the secret of Arthur's Knights to you, and your issue," whispered the Wizard.

"What are my issue and what do you know of my unicorn?" asked Shariff.

"Your issue means your children and your children's children for evermore. As for the unicorn you wear around your neck it was I who first gave it to your ancestor Hakim "

With that Merlin struck the rock with his twisted staff and the chasm opened once again as it had done all those years before revealing the iron gates.

"Follow me." commanded Merlin and Shariff clutching the unicorn medallion tightly followed the Wizard deep into the cave until they arrived in the cavern, where the slumbering knights lay with their milk white steeds.

Shariff was amazed at the sight and knew instinctively that there was very powerful magic at work in that place.

Merlin rested on his strange staff and began to relate the tale to Shariff.

"These knights have slumbered here for a thousand years. They are ready to leap to the defence of this realm in its hour of need. Eight hundred years ago your ancestor Hakim the Saracen came here to deliver the Holy Grail from Jerusalem and they have slumbered here until today. Your ancestors have been guardians of the biggest secret since the passing of Jesus Christ and without knowing it, have set an example of truth and honour which would serve the World well, if they but knew. The Silver unicorn was passed to you by your uncle Hussain and you used it when you were in danger. What I have to tell you is that the unicorn will protect you and your descendants for as long as you keep the secret of the Grail.

You have already proved your bravery and trustworthiness as did your kinsmen entrusted with the secret over the centuries. Carry the unicorn with pride and pass it on when you are ready to leave this world. It is your families rightful reward for faithful service to a religion which is not your own."

Shariff was still puzzled by the explanation Merlin had given and asked "What is the Holy Grail?"

Merlin showed him the grail saying "This is the drinking vessel which some believe that Jesus Christ drank from at the last supper with his twelve disciples. Some people also believe that when Christ was crucified Mary Magdalene caught drops of his blood from where the legionary had pierced his side with a spear. It is a holy relic beyond price and will now reside here for eternity and never be allowed to fall into the wrong hands of people who would misuse it for their personal gain"

With that Merlin turned to leave the cave and Shariff followed him. On the way out the Wizard filled Shariff's pockets and bag with gold coins and jewels.

When they reached the sunlight again the old man walked away leaning heavily on his staff and gradually disappeared into the trees. Shariff watched the wizard go and when he turned around, the entrance to the cave had mysteriously vanished.

Shariff knew that it was time to find the others before he was missed and hurried along the path in the direction which they had taken. Soon he had caught the rest of the class up and Mr Burton made a joke about spending a penny in the woods and Mr Garnet said he thought Shariff might have been spirited away inside the earth by the Wizard of Alderley Edge.

Strangely although he knew he had been missing for ages the others thought that he had only been gone for a short while. More of Merlin's magic at work Sharrif had little doubt.

He now knew that it was possible for things to happen which had no rational explanation and he realised that some people were gifted with talents which could not be believed unless you had seen them with your own eyes.

Shariff just smiled and said nothing. The secrets of Alderley Edge were safe with him as they had been since the time of his ancestor Hakim the original Dark Man of Biddulph Moor.

When they had explored the rest of Alderley Edge they all said goodbye to Mr Garnet and climbed into the mini-bus for the short journey back to Macclesfield.

Mr Burton was in a very jolly mood and sang all the way back to school and Rani knew why. She had noticed Miss smiling at him when he shared his chocolate with her and she thought that romance was truly blossoming between them.

When they got back to school they learned that Mrs Herbert had suspended Wayne and his two cronies for a week and that she had reported matters to the school governors and to the education offices in Chester.

 The next morning was Saturday and when Shariff was woken by his two brothers he suddenly felt happier than he had for months. He reviewed all the events of the past few days in his head and could scarcely believe everything which had happened to him. When he came down the stairs for breakfast he was extremely surprised to see his father still sitting in the kitchen. Saturday was usually his Father's busiest day with the taxi and he had usually left the house long before Shariff rose.

"Hello Father are you still here?"

"Yes indeed I am and I have a surprise for you Shariff." Replied his father waving two slips of paper in his hand.

"What have you there father?"

"These, my boy, are tickets for this afternoons football match compliments of Crewe Alexandra FC. They have heard about your bravery and found that you are a fan of their opponents today. They have sent two tickets to the Director's box and you are to meet the teams after the match. Well what do you think about that?

Shariff was speechless but the grin which spread across his face said all that his father needed to know.

THE CAVE ALDERLEY EDGE

Historical Background Research

Biddulph is an Old Saxon name and its descendants can trace their ancestors back to Saxon roots.

The name Biddulph means wolf killer Bid (killer) wulf (wolf).

A name of much kudos as hunting wolves was a dangerous sport which required skill and courage.

After the Norman Conquest in 1066 the land was divided and given to the Noblemen who had fought with William the Conqueror at the battle of Hastings.

The most powerful Norman landowner in Staffordshire Robert de Stafford, a relative of the Conqueror.

> This Robert held no less than one hundred and fifty lordships at the time of Domesday, of which more than half lay in Staffordshire, including Norton-in-the-moors, Chell, Madeley, Burslem, Hulton, and Rushton, in the immediate neighbourhood. He, with his brother Nigel, came in with the Conqueror, whose kinsmen they were, and he liberally rewarded both out of the spoils of the English proprietors.

> The devastating vengeance which William inflicted on the Saxon revolters, may probably account for the immense tract of waste lands in Staffordshire, mentioned in Domesday, where about thirty lordships are specified in succession, including Biddulph, Endon, Bucknall, Shelton Cheadle and its vicinity; to which list is added the ...observation "All this land of the King is waste!"

Alfred Fitz Ormius was the grandson of a Norman Richard the Forrester who according to the Domesday Book had 10 Lordships in north Staffordshire. He was given the Saxon heiress of the manor of Biddulph to marry when he was aged just 16. Ormus de Guidon was the son of Richard the Forrester and succeeded him in all his possessions. Ormus lived through the reigns of William II, Henry I and Stephen and was a supporter of Henry II.

The land at Knypersley passed to Alured (Alfred) from his father Ormius. The eldest son Robert inherited the estates at Darlaston near Stone in Staffordshire.

The setting for our tale begins during the third Crusade to the Holy Land. The third Crusade 1189-1192 was led by King Henry II of England and Philip II of France. When Henry II died early in the campaign Richard I, The Lionheart took command. In 1192 King Richard and Saladin finalized a treaty by which Jerusalem would remain under Muslim control, but which also allowed unarmed Christian pilgrims to visit the city.

It must be remembered that although Richard the Lionheart was king of England he was born and raised in France and refused to speak English. He only spent six months of his reign in England.

Meanwhile his brother John took full advantage of his brother's absence.

The story of the 3rd Crusade is well documented in the Ridley Scott film "Kingdom of Heaven."

It is thought that Alured Fitz Ormius (Fitz means son of) inherited the Lordship of the manor on his return from the crusade in 1195 and changed his name to Alfred de Kuipersley.

Alured was the son of Ormius and the grandson of Richard the Forrester who was a tenant in chief of William the Conqueror and the Keeper of Cannock Chase a royal deer park. At that time Cannock Chase extended as far north as the Moorland. It is believed that Richard the Forrester was a Saxon and the largest non Norman landholder in the whole of England.

Ormius or "Orme de Derlaston" or "Orm le Guiden", otherwise known as Orm of Biddulph was a major figure. He held manors through the county from Biddulph to Essington. Stafford would have been in the centre of his land and it is believed he built St Chads church in Stafford. His wife was the daughter of Nicholas de Beauchamp Lord of Chartley Castle.

Alured is reputed to have returned from the 3rd Crusade with a Saracen servant. This Saracen was granted the position of Bailiff of Biddulph Moor which was part of the Manor of Knypersley.

On Biddulph Moor is to be found the spring which is the source of the River Trent.

The valley of Knypersley is now submerged beneath a reservoir which supplies the Cauldon Canal with water; the land around it is a country park.

To this day there exists on Biddulph Moor and surrounding areas a race of people who are physically different to others. They possess a brown skin and auburn hair. They are said to inherit these characteristics from the Saracen and the local girl he took for his wife. Interestingly many of these Dark Men of Biddulph retain the surname of Bailey said to stem from the fact that the Saracen was made a Bailiff of Biddulph Moor by his master

Centuries later in 1483 a descendant of the Knypersley family one Ralph Rudyerd is said to have killed Richard II at Bosworth Field so helping to establish the Tudor dynasty.

"Orme de Derlaston" or "Orm le Guiden", otherwise known as Ormius of Biddulph, who was a major figure. He held manors through the county from Biddulph to Essington. Stafford would have been in the centre of his land. His father was Richard the Forester, the Keeper of Cannock Chase and what was called the New Forest, which was a position of immense power over everything that happened in the forest. At that time the forest extended all the way to the moorlands. St Chad's carvings show forest animals, deer in the trees. Richard was one of the largest non-Norman landowners in the Doomsday Book.

In 1150 (when he was probably an old man) Ormius held manors from Biddluph and Knypersley to Essington, and most places between. Stafford was the only town of any size in this area, and the obvious place to found a church. It is possible that his wife was the daughter of Nicholas de Tosny, Lord of Stafford Castle, making him closely related to Norman royalty, though others claim his father-in-law was Nicholas de Beauchamp of Chartley Castle.

There are no records of Orm's death, but he and his wife claimed the right to be buried at Burton Abbey "with great honour". His family continues to hold some of his land to this day! Direct descendants
through the line of his son Edward still live at Okeover near Ilam.

1195 state documents show a deed bestowing "Gny-presley", to one named Alfred Fitz Ormius: he changes his name to Alfred de Kuipersley; builds Great Hall, close to site of present Hall, he also becomes a very wealthy man
1206 Royal Warrant issued for creation of Royal Deer Park at Knypersley of 250 acres, adjacent to the Great Hall
1216 Alfred de Kuipersley's death, his son William de Kuiteleqe succeeds to The Manor
1285 A Royal licence issued for the hunting and killing of all wild wolves roaming the Biddulph area
1295 Allan de Kuipersley, aged 15 years is murdered in the deer-park, his assassins are never caught
1314 A Royal licence is again issued to hunt and kill wolves roaming in the deer-park at Kuipersley.
1350 Bubonic Plaque lack Death) in the Biddulph Valley, many families become extinct
1356 Richard de Shidyeard (Sherratt) is outlawed from the county, for the murder of Richard and Vincent de Kuipersley, this took place at Kuipersly Vale (now Knypersley pool)